IF FOUND PLEASE RETURN

👤 _____

✉ _____

📱 _____

Greater Than a Tourist Book Series
Reviews from Readers

I think the series is wonderful and beneficial for tourists to get information before visiting the city.

-Seckin Zumbul, Izmir Turkey

I am a world traveler who has read many trip guides but this one really made a difference for me. I would call it a heartfelt creation of a local guide expert instead of just a guide.

-Susy, Isla Holbox, Mexico

New to the area like me, this is a must have!

-Joe, Bloomington, USA

This is a good series that gets down to it when looking for things to do at your destination without having to read a novel for just a few ideas.

-Rachel, Monterey, USA

Good information to have to plan my trip to this destination.

-Pennie Farrell, Mexico

Great ideas for a port day.

-Mary Martin USA

Aptly titled, you won't just be a tourist after reading this book. You'll be greater than a tourist!

-Alan Warner, Grand Rapids, USA

Even though I only have three days to spend in San Miguel in an upcoming visit, I will use the author's suggestions to guide some of my time there. An easy read - with chapters named to guide me in directions I want to go.

 -Robert Catapano, USA

Great insights from a local perspective! Useful information and a very good value!

 -Sarah, USA

This series provides an in-depth experience through the eyes of a local. Reading these series will help you to travel the city in with confidence and it'll make your journey a unique one.

-Andrew Teoh, Ipoh, Malaysia

GREATER THAN A TOURIST- SAINT PAUL MINNESOTA USA

50 Travel Tips from a Local

Charlie Enders

Cover designed by: Ivana Stamenkovic
Cover Image: https://pixabay.com/en/saint-paul-minnesota-140199/

CZYK Publishing Since 2011.

Greater Than a Tourist
Visit our website at www.GreaterThanaTourist.com

Lock Haven, PA
All rights reserved.
ISBN: 9781724131010

>TOURIST

50 TRAVEL TIPS FROM A LOCAL

BOOK DESCRIPTION

Are you excited about planning your next trip?

Do you want to try something new?

Would you like some guidance from a local?

If you answered yes to any of these questions, then this Greater Than a Tourist book is for you.

Greater Than a Tourist- Saint Paul by Charlie Enders offers the inside scoop on Minnesota's capital city. Most travel books tell you how to travel like a tourist. Although there is nothing wrong with that, as part of the Greater Than a Tourist series, this book will give you travel tips from someone who has lived at your next travel destination.

In these pages, you will discover advice that will help you throughout your stay. This book will not tell you exact addresses or store hours but instead will give you excitement and knowledge from a local that you may not find in other smaller print travel books.

Travel like a local. Slow down, stay in one place, and get to know the people and the culture. By the time you finish this book, you will be eager and prepared to travel to your next destination.

TABLE OF CONTENTS

14. State Capitol
15. Grand Avenue
16. The Lexington
17. Grand Old Creamery
18. Grand Old Day
19. West 7th Street
20. Summit Brewing Company
21. Mancini's
22. Cossetta
23. Mickey's Diner
24. Xcel Energy Center
25. Children's Museum

SPORTS AND ENTERTAINMENT

26. Fitzgerald Theater
27. The Ordway
28. Palace Theater
29. Como Zoo
30. Saints Game (CHS Field)
31. Highland National Golf Course
32. Saint Paul Curling Club
33. Indian Mounds Regional Park
34. Crosby Farm Regional Park
35. Fort Snelling State Park
36. Lake Phalen
37. Rice Park
38. Harriet Island

DEDICATION

This book is dedicated to the actual Saint Paul, the patron saint of writing (among other things). You probably didn't know you'd have an amazing city named after you someday, but thank you nonetheless.

ABOUT THE AUTHOR

Charlie Enders is a freelance writer who lives in Saint Paul. He loves to play ultimate, play with dogs, and play (in general). While he was raised in the suburbs, he attended high school at Cretin-Derham Hall in Saint Paul and fell in love with the city's character and history. He's lucky enough to now call it home.

HOW TO USE THIS BOOK

The Greater Than a Tourist book series was written by someone who has lived in an area for over three months. The goal of this book is to help travelers either dream or experience different locations by providing opinions from a local. The author has made suggestions based on their own experiences. Please do your own research before traveling to the area in case the suggested places are unavailable.

FROM THE PUBLISHER

Traveling can be one of the most important parts of a person's life. The anticipation and memories that you have are some of the best. As a publisher of the Greater Than a Tourist book series, as well as the popular 50 Things to Know book series, we strive to help you learn about new places, spark your imagination, and inspire you. Wherever you are and whatever you do I wish you safe, fun, and inspiring travel.

Lisa Rusczyk Ed. D.
CZYK Publishing

OUR STORY

Traveling is a passion of the "Greater than a Tourist" series creator. Lisa studied abroad in college, and for their honeymoon Lisa and her husband toured Europe. During her travels to Malta, an older man tried to give her some advice based on his own experience living on the island since he was a young boy. She was not sure if she should talk to the stranger but was interested in his advice. When traveling to some places she was wary to talk to locals because she was afraid that they weren't being genuine. Through her travels, Lisa learned how much locals had to share with tourists. Lisa created the "Greater Than a Tourist" book series to help connect people with locals. A topic that locals are very passionate about sharing.

WELCOME TO
> TOURIST

INTRODUCTION

"I don't say I was the first,
because, who knows, maybe there
was a guy out in Minnesota doing it
before me."

-Don Rickles

While perhaps the less-heralded of the Twin Cities, what Saint Paul lacks in size it makes up for in character. From the state capitol to the guy jet skiing on Lake Phalen, Saint Paul oozes personality from its every nook and cranny. All you have to know is the best places to find it- and that's where I come in! In the pages ahead you'll get an in-depth walkthrough of everything I've learned, experienced, and loved about Saint Paul for the last two decades. And this is only scratching the surface!

Let's start with the most important thing: your appetite.

13

FOOD

Now, a look through any online food directory might cause overload for the average schmuck- but you're not the average schmuck (because you're reading his book). Before you gorge yourself at the first food truck you see, have a plan- what do you like? What are you in the mood for? Are you looking for three square meals a day or do you prefer snacking? It might sound like minutia but these are the questions that will make or break your dining experience.

1. MAKE SURE YOU HAVE AN EMPTY STOMACH

Most important to remember is this: Saint Paul is filled to the brim with delectable things to ingest, so make sure you don't just fill up on bread (so to speak). You're going to want to try as much as possible; from Juicy Lucys to Sweet Martha's. You'd be doing yourself a disservice to not prepare your stomach accordingly.

2. THE NOOK

And there's no place better to begin your culinary tour of STP than at Casper and Runyon's Nook, located in historic Mac-Groveland. With walls adorned with decades of awards and laudations, the Nook doesn't try to hide its sterling reputation. Nor should it; one bite of a Juicy Lucy- an exquisitely tender burger filled with cheese- and you'll be hooked. Head downstairs and enjoy the attached bowling alley or take a stroll around adjacent Cretin-Derham Hall High School's gorgeous grounds for some after-meal fun.

3. MERITAGE

If you're in the mood for a swanky date night out on the town, the preeminent destination in Saint Paul is the incredibly opulent Meritage. If you don't mind shelling out the money, you and your special somebody will love it- the grandiose oyster, delectable dishes, and especially the Northern hemisphere-focused wine list. Grab a glass of rose and look out at gorgeous downtown as you enjoy the weather up on the terrace- it doesn't get much better!

4. PAZZALUNA

Look, I don't know about you, but I love Italian food. When I'm eating pasta I'm on cloud nine- and nowhere is that more true than at Pazzaluna, located in the heart of downtown. Executive Chef Michele Totaro spent years honing his craft in Italy, Tokyo, and Hong Kong- that experience gives Pazzaluna a menu unlike any other. If you're heading to a play at the Ordway or a Wild game at the X, this is a fantastic stop for drinks and apps as well- you don't have to get the famous gnocchi to appreciate Pazzaluna!

PLACES TO SEE

Times a-wasting! You've got important things to do and places to see- make sure you have a plan and attack it like you would a Juicy Lucy at the Nook!

5. THE SAINT PAUL HOTEL

While there are endless options available both in and around the city, for a uniquely Saint Paul experience you'll want to stay at the Saint Paul Hotel. As the city's most historic hotel, countless celebrities, dignitaries, and people of import have stayed within

17

its timeless walls- and the staff will make you feel just as important when you're a guest. Besides the hotel's 255 elegantly appointed guest rooms and suites, it also boasts an impossibly elegant restaurant on its ground floor: The Saint Paul Grill. You could stay in the hotel, lose track of time, and never once leave throughout your stay- not that I recommend that, of course; there's just too much else to do and see!

6. GETTING AROUND

Once you manage to pry yourself away from the hotel, you'll want a quick and cheap way to get around. Just hop aboard the light-rail and take a cruise down University Avenue! The Green Line goes from Union Depot (see below) to Target Field in downtown Minneapolis, stopping at every major intersection along the way. For shorter trips, there are dozens of Nice Ride Bike Station scattered throughout the city. Rent for a single ride or a full day of exploration- at $6 you won't find a better deal anywhere!

7. UNION DEPOT

Originally constructed in 1881, Union Depot was lovingly restored in 2011 and is now a major hub for Midwest commuters. Whether you're hopping onto the Green Line and heading to a Twins game or settling into an Amtrak for a cross-country adventure, Union Depot provides a gorgeous and memorable venue for visitors.

8. RAMSEY HOUSE

For an inside look into the Saint Paul of yore, take a tour of the stately Alexander Ramsey House. As the former residence of Alexander Ramsey, the first governor of Minnesota Territory and the second governor of the state of Minnesota, the house is brimming with authentic amenities and furnishing from when Minnesota was young and Saint Paul was called Pig's Eye (little trivia for you). Take the family on an educational afternoon- even if they complain, it'll be good for them!

9. MINNESOTA HISTORY CENTER

If you want a more all-encompassing look through the history of Saint Paul (and Minnesota in general), don't overthink it- the Minnesota History Center is a fantastic place to spend a few hours. Peruse through the many inspiring exhibits and learn about everything Minnesota, from its humble beginnings to the many ways the Mississippi River has influenced its growth and development. There are plenty of activities to keep kids amused as well!

10. SCIENCE MUSEUM

A trip to Saint Paul isn't complete without a visit to what is perhaps the single best museum in the state. The Minnesota Science Museum was founded in 1907, and its stately visage on the banks of the Mississippi River contains more than 370,000 square feet of world-class exhibits. Those include a 10,000-square-foot temporary exhibit gallery, five permanent galleries, acres of outdoor space, and an Imax Convertible Dome Omnitheater, which stretches over your head for a one-of-a-kind immersive experience.

Over a million people from around the globe visit the museum- you'd be remiss if you weren't one of them!

11. SUMMIT AVENUE

If you're an architecture buff, you'd be hard-pressed to find a better place to take a stroll than historic Summit Avenue. Known for being the longest avenue of Victorian homes in the country, Summit stretches four and a half miles from downtown Saint Paul to the edge of Minneapolis. Tours are offered through the Minnesota Historical Society if you'd prefer a more guided experience!

12. JAMES J HILL HOUSE

If the Alexander Ramsey House wasn't quite enough for your inner history nerd, the James J Hill House should be next on your to-do list. This gargantuan stone mansion is the most famous stop on Summit, and a shining example of Gilded Age architecture. Originally owned by rail tycoon James J. Hill, the house features 13 bathrooms, 22 fireplaces, 16 chandeliers, a nearly 100-foot long reception hall, sophisticated technical systems, and a two-story,

21

skylit art gallery. You don't have to love history (the house was built in 1891) to appreciate the sublime design and luxurious rooms of this National Historic Landmark. Bring the kids, a date, or just yourself if you have even a passing interest in Saint Paul history.

13. THE CATHEDRAL

Continue along Summit and eventually the road will end at the base of a towering gothic structure. Designed by E. L. Masqueray, the Cathedral of Saint Paul's cornerstone was back in 1907, and it's been a signature landmark ever since. After a tour of the majestic interior, step out onto the granite steps and enjoy a sublime view of the neighboring...

14. STATE CAPITOL

It's tough to find a spot in downtown where you CAN'T see this magnificent building. Hop into a free guided tour and learn not just about the building but about the great State of Minnesota itself. You'll get a first-hand look at the famous domed central chamber, the governor's office, and even the gold leaf gilded horse statue on the balcony.

15. GRAND AVENUE

Of course, with all that learning you're going to want to let loose afterwards, and there's no better place to do so than Grand. Generally accepted as Saint Paul's "place to be on the weekend", Grand Avenue is filled to the brim with unique restaurants, unforgettable bars, and hundreds of places to shop. Get your credit card in hand and limber up your shoulders, 'cause you'll be carrying some heavy bags at the end of the day!

16. THE LEXINGTON

The Lexington is a step back into the turn of the 20th century. Named for its location on the corner of Lexington Parkway and Grand Avenue, The Lexington opened in 1935 right after the end of prohibition. While it initially was a bar for locals to simply enjoy themselves, The Lexington has evolved into one of the city's finest restaurants, without losing the sociability it made its name on.

17. GRAND OLD CREAMERY

Walk by The Grand Ole Creamery and you'll be punched in the face with the delicious aroma of homemade, hand-rolled, malted waffle cones. And what goes in those delectable cones but some of the finest, tastiest ice cream in the state (or world). On hot summer days the line stretches out the door at this Grand Avenue hot spot, and for good reason. Over 200 different flavors, hot pizza, and friendly service have made countless lifelong customers out of the locals. And don't worry- the line moves fast!

18. GRAND OLD DAY

If you're lucky enough to be in town on the first Sunday in June, you're in for a treat- Grand Old Day is Saint Paul's unofficial summer kickoff celebration. Taking place entirely along (where else) Grand Avenue, the festival features over 150 food vendors, plus concerts, beer, and general merriment. It's the perfect way to experience just why Grand Avenue is so unique!

19. WEST 7TH STREET

Historic West 7th is known, primarily, for its stupendous dining opportunities, all of which are best enjoyed before or after an event in downtown. Besides the food, the street features some of the most historic homes in the Irvine Park neighborhood, plus unique shops, a growing art scene, and Saint Paul's first craft brewery- Summit Brewery.

20. SUMMIT BREWING COMPANY

Minnesota is known for its craft breweries, and Summit is one of its best. As the 25th largest craft brewer in the U.S., Summit produced approximately 115,000 barrels of beer in 2017- delicious, hoppy, golden beer. Stop in for a $5 tour of the brewery, plus a flight of four 7-oz. beers- and afterwards head outside for a game of corn hole. You'll see what all the fuss is about!

21. MANCINI'S

Mancini's Char House first opened its doors back in 1948- are you noticing a trend yet? Saint Paul is a town with a rich history and numerous timeless places to eat and things to see. Mancini's is no exception. Since the Mancini family took over in 1968, they've prided themselves on great food and service with a personal touch. Mancini's also knows that some of the finest steakhouses in the world are located in Italy- but it's their job to prove it to you! Cut into a carefully raised and aged steak, grilled on a huge open-hearth charcoal pit and you'll be a marbled meaty heaven.

22. COSSETTA

If Italian food is more your style, head down west 7th street and stop at Cossetta Alimentari. Recently expanded to keep up with demand, Cossetta specializes in humongous pieces of pizza and their world-famous mostaccioli. But that's not all! Attached to the eatery you'll find a smörgåsbord of edible delights: Bar Louis is available if you're looking for a more upscale, rooftop experience, while the attached market is filled to the brim with authentic

Italian products for purchase. Before you leave, make sure you grab some gelato or a cannoli from the pasticceria- it's just the cherry on top of an unforgettable experience!

23. MICKEY'S DINER

Drive along West 7th past the X and you'll see something that looks pretty out of place- an old fashioned dining car. While the city around it has changed, Mickey's remains just as charming and delicious as it was in 1945. The diner is open 24/7 365 days a year- so feel free to stop by for pancakes, a burger, and/or a malt whenever you like! Fun fact- Mickey's has been seen and featured in three big-budget films: A Prairie Home Companion, Jingle All the Way, and the enduring classic The Mighty Ducks.

24. XCEL ENERGY CENTER

Like hockey? Is it winter? If you said yes to both, get your behind to the Xcel Energy Center for a Wild game. The stadium is vintage Minnesota, and is consistently ranked near the top of "Best Pro Stadium" lists. If you answered no to either of those questions, how about concerts? The X is also a sublime venue to see some of the biggest stars in the world, bringing in everyone from Paul McCartney to Prince.

25. CHILDREN'S MUSEUM

Got kids? Well, the Minnesota Children's Museum should be a no-brainer. Founded with the philosophy that there would be no "do not touch" signs in the museum, kids are encouraged to explore and touch to their heart's content. Among the most popular exhibits are the crane and giant anthill- children can enter the muskrat lodge and pretend to be a busy beaver, crawl under the 500-gallon aquarium, challenge your balancing skills at the bouldering wall, come face-to-face with turtles, make waves at the wild water table or turn a gooey mess into paper art. It's a month's worth of fun condensed into an afternoon- and as a bonus, it's educational!

SPORTS AND ENTERTAINMENT

The Twin Cities have a thriving theater scene, with numerous venues for musicals, drama, music, and more. They also have some sports teams, but I wouldn't refer to them as "thriving".

26. FITZGERALD THEATER

Let's start with the oldest active theatre in Saint Paul. The Fitz is the home of American Public Media's Live from Here, (formerly named A Prairie Home Companion), and has been a Saint Paul institution for decades. Besides Chris Thile's variety show there are regular concerts and events held within its gilded walls- but even if you aren't attending one you'd be doing yourself a disservice if you didn't stop in and just have a look around!

27. THE ORDWAY

For the highest quality dramatic theater in the cities, The Ordway Center for the Performing Arts has no equal. While touring Broadway musicals

29

sometimes stop by, the theater is famous for its orchestra, opera, and cultural performers- many of which are native to Minnesota. The Minnesota Opera, Saint Paul Chamber Orchestra, and The Schubert Club all call it home- and for a night on the town you can't do much better.

28. PALACE THEATER

Rounding out the trifecta of downtown theaters, the Palace is where you'll find live music on a weekly basis. Although the venue dates back to 1916, the Palace was completely renovated in 2016. The first show at the renovated theater was Atmosphere, The Jayhawks, and Phantogram- relax in the vintage cushioned seats as you take in a show!

29. COMO ZOO

One of the most popular destinations on a hot summer afternoon, the Como Zoo was the first zoo established in Minnesota and remains a Saint Paul institution. Founded in 1897, the zoo has gone through numerous transformations and renovations over the years- the most recent of which is the zoo's newest exhibit: Gorilla Forest. Inside the jungle habitat is Schroeder the 500-pound silverback male, three female companions, and a bachelor group of three other males. After that, make your way over to Seal Island, the Tropical Encounters Exhibit, Polar Bear Odyssey, or any one of the multiple other incredible exhibits. And the best part- it's totally free (although donations are definitely appreciated)!

30. SAINTS GAME (CHS FIELD)

Ever seen Space Jam? Of course you have. Remember the hat that Bill Murray wears throughout the film? Well it just so happens that that hat is a Saint Paul Saints Hat- and Bill Murray is a part owner of the team. CHS Field, opened in April 2015, is the Saint's gorgeous 7,210 seat ballpark, located in Lowertown. If you like baseball but are also looking for a less serious, family focused atmosphere, a Saint's game is ideal. The baseball is great, the entertainment is varied and hilarious, and the venue is second to none!

31. HIGHLAND NATIONAL GOLF COURSE

Grab your clubs and take a swing at one of the most famous courses in the Twin Cities! Highland National Golf Course, recently renovated in 2005, is smack dab in the middle of the gorgeous Mac-Groveland and Highland neighborhoods. Speckled along its 18 Par 72 Length are aged oaks, verdant grass, and, perhaps most famously, large "Snoopy" shaped bunker on the 15th. Peanuts creator Charles Schultz actually learned to play golf here- make sure you do him proud!

32. SAINT PAUL CURLING CLUB

Ever watch the winter Olympics and wonder where the US' many incredible curlers come from? First established in 1885, the Saint Paul Curling Club maintains the largest active membership (for curling clubs) in the country, with over 1200 registered members. While only members can actually play, guests are welcome to watch live curling games in the heated club room and upstairs bar area.

PARKS

Saint Paul has a wide variety of parks scattered throughout the city- downtown, Mac-Groveland, lowertown, Highland... if you're looking to get closer to mother nature you never have far to go.

33. INDIAN MOUNDS REGIONAL PARK

Indian Mounds Regional Park, so named for the six Native American burial mounds found within, offers a unique perspective on the city. And by unique perspective, I mean that it offers a sweeping view of both the Mississippi River and downtown, from high atop 450 million-year-old limestone and sandstone bluffs. If that doesn't sound enticing enough, there's also a biking/hiking trail, picnic areas, and even some public art. We're a classy sort, here in a Saint Paul.

34. CROSBY FARM REGIONAL PARK

So named for Thomas Crosby- an English immigrant who staked out 160 acres in the valley southwest of the present-day junction of Shepard

Road and Interstate 35E in 1858- Crosby Farm is the premier park to enjoy the famous Mississippi River. If you're interested in biking, walking, or running, there are 6.7 miles of paved trail adjacent to the river, along shady, wooded terrain. Got a fishing license? Cast off into Crosby Lake, Upper Lake, or the Mississippi itself! While the lakes are mostly filled with panfish, the river is a great place to plumb for walleyes, sauger, northern pike and muskie- the quintessential Minnesota fish!

35. FORT SNELLING STATE PARK

Take a step back into the 1800's at historic Fort Snelling (or Bdote, as it was known to the Dakota). This reconstructed fort offers an authentic old timey experience, with in-character actors and enthusiastic tour guides everywhere you look. Learn about the Dakota, the role Fort Snelling played in the US-Dakota War of 1862, and even what day to day life was like back in the mid-19th century.

Once you've had your fill of Fort Snelling's historic side, head down to the actual state park for a little rest and relaxation. There are canoes and kayaks available for rent, wildlife to observe, and a swimming beach to cool off in. An insider's tip- in the summer, head to the state park once it's dark. It's maybe the best place to see fireflies in the state!

36. LAKE PHALEN

Fort Snelling's beach is great, but the premier place hit the sand is, without a doubt, Phalen. Lake Phalen is one of the largest in the city, and its expansive sand beach is the perfect place to soak up some rays, build a sandcastle, or sprint into the lake's cerulean waters from. Got 300 friends? Phalen's picnic pavilion can accommodate all of them. If you're looking for something more unique, there are also sailing lessons, free exercise programs, and tennis courts.

37. RICE PARK

Saint Paul's equivalent of Central Park, Rice Park is located in the heart of downtown. While there are numerous festivals, concerts and events located here throughout the year, it's a must-visit come winter time. During the colder months the Wells Fargo WinterSkate is open- a free place to skate around in an oval while you enjoy the sights and sounds found only in downtown Saint Paul. No skates? No problem- rentals are free as well. The park also features a beautiful fountain and is adjacent to the Saint Paul Hotel, Landmark Center, Ordway and the Downtown Central Library. Make a day of it and visit them all!

38. HARRIET ISLAND

There are dozens of ways to enjoy an afternoon in Harriet Island Regional Park. It's pristine location along the banks of the Mississippi and adjacent to downtown gives it superior views of the gorgeous Saint Paul skyline, while the island itself boasts numerous amenities for couples and families to enjoy. But if you're looking for a truly unique way to experience the area, hop aboard one of the ferries for a trip along the longest "natural road" in the country. Keep your eyes open for bald eagles, herons, egrets, and falcons as you journey into Mississippi National Great River Park and back (eventually).

FESTIVALS, FAIRS, AND EVENTS

One of Saint Paul's defining features is its famous festivals. While the big kahuna is obviously the state fair, there are dozens of other, smaller, but just as interesting events to visit, attend, or participate in. These are just a few!

39. FARMERS MARKET

Located in lowertown right next to CHS Field, the Farmers Market is open in late summer and fall every Saturday morning and features an assortment of fresh fruits, veggies, and more. Minnesota is known for its many varieties of apples, squash and sweet corn, but the farmer's market is also about people. Strike up a conversation with a farmer and they'll be more than happy to discuss their product, the weather, or how poorly the Vikings played last Sunday.

40. STATE FAIR

Hooooooo boy. If you're in town for the two weeks before Labor Day, you're in for a treat. The State Fair could merit a guide by itself (in fact, it has dozens), but I'll do my best to condense it down into a tight couple of paragraphs.

The State Fair is known, first and foremost, for its food. More specifically, it's weird and incredibly unhealthy food. Big Fat Bacon on a Stick, deep fried Twinkies, cheese curds, and the piece de resistance, Sweet Martha's Cookies... the list is nigh endless. Think of a food right now and add "on a stick" to the end of it. That's probably available somewhere at the State Fair. Not kidding.

Second, the State Fair is known for its incredible popularity. If you want an experience that isn't hindered by a veritable sea of bodies, avoid weekends like the plague. Mornings and evenings on weekdays are ideal if you want survivable crowds and a full fair experience.

The fair has numerous other things to do and see, from the agriculture building to the grandstand to the Midway. Stop in the animal barns and see some pigs, chickens, cows, turkeys, sheep, and even the Miracle of Birth Center, which is exactly what it sounds like.

46. THE WABASHA STREET CAVES

I've mentioned the word "unique" a fair amount on this list, but it doesn't get any unique-ier than this. Natural (but somewhat modified) caves adjacent to downtown, the Wabasha Street Caves have served a variety of purposes over the years. It was originally used by native tribes before settlers arrived in the area, but once they arrived in the 1840's they began mining the cave's natural silica for glass making. After that, it was a mushroom farm in the early 1900s, a speakeasy during the days of prohibition, and finally a disco in the 70s. Today the caves continue to be an event spot, with the notable caveat of potentially being haunted by murdered gangsters and speakeasy patrons. But don't be afraid- cave tours are conducted on Mondays, Thursdays, and on weekends.

47. THE PEOPLE!

If you haven't heard the term "Minnesota Nice" before, you'll know what it means by the time you leave. Strike up a conversation with a bartender, a tour guide, or just a regular Joe on the street and you'll more often than not be treated to a conversation. Keep your ears open for "You betcha" and "Oofda"- both are notorious Minnesota mannerisms.

48. PEANUTS STATUES

Spend enough time walking around the Twin Cities and a feeling of déjà vu will start to creep in. Five foot tall statues depicting various characters from Peanuts- on street corners, in shopping malls, and just on the side of the street, smiling and decorated with a theme in mind. After the death of Charles Schulz in 2000, artists from all over the Twin Cities designed and displayed renditions of Peanuts characters, beginning with Snoopy but eventually also including Charlie Brown, Lucy, Linus, and a version of Snoopy with Woodstock. There are over 100 statues scattered throughout the Twin Cities- make sure you keep an eye open!

49. LARGE GREEN CHAIR

Don't overthink it- this is exactly what it sounds like. Originally built in 1995 and located in High Bridge Park, the present big green chair replaced the original in 2002 after weathering destroyed it. But why, you might ask, is there a big green chair? Was it for Paul Bunyan? Sadly no, but happily, it's for an awesome reason. The Large Green Chair was made as a publicity piece for The Green Chair Project, which employs inner city youth over the summer constructing and marketing regular-sized green Adirondack lawn chairs. However, you'll probably just want to take a picture with it- all 2500 pounds.

50. MINNEAPOLIS

Maybe this is against the rules, but Saint Paul and Minneapolis are known as "the Twin Cities" for a reason. Minneapolis doesn't have the historical charm of Saint Paul, but it IS the biggest city in the state, and has innumerable things for you to experience should you have your fill of the state capital. Twins games at Target Field, Vikings games at US Bank, nightlife in downtown, breweries in Northeast, walks around Lake Nokomis or Lake Bde Maka Ska... add in that Minneapolis is one of the most biker-friendly cities in the country and you have a package that's hard to turn down. That is, of course, once you've exhausted everything you could possibly do in Saint Paul, which- if you read this guide thoroughly- will take a long time!

.

TOP REASONS TO BOOK THIS TRIP

The History: From the James J Hill House to the History Center to the numerous restaurants that have hung around for a century, Saint Paul's history is everywhere you look- if that interests you (and it should) you won't want to go anywhere else.

The Food: Juicy Lucy's, cheese curds, lutefisk, lefse, hotdish, numerous ice creameries... I could go on, but it'd be quicker if you just came and sampled them yourself.

The Places you'll go!: Start the day at the Farmer's Market, then hit the Science Museum, then the Children's Museum, a Saints or Wild Game, then head back to the Saint Paul Hotel and Grill for a nightcap under the stars. Sounds pretty good, right?

BONUS BOOK

50 THINGS TO KNOW ABOUT PACKING LIGHT FOR TRAVEL

PACK THE RIGHT WAY EVERY TIME

AUTHOR: MANIDIPA BHATTACHARYYA

Edited by Melanie Howthorne

ABOUT THE AUTHOR

Manidipa Bhattacharyya is a creative writer and editor, with an education in English literature and Linguistics. After working in the IT industry for seven long years she decided to call it quits and follow her heart instead. Manidipa has been ghost writing, editing, proof reading and doing secondary research services for many story tellers and article writers for about three years. She stays in Kolkata, India with her husband and a busy two year old. In her own time Manidipa enjoys travelling, photography and writing flash fiction.

Manidipa believes in travelling light and never carries anything that she couldn't haul herself on a trip. However, travelling with her child changed the scenario. She seemed to carry the entire world with her for the baby on the first two trips. But good sense prevailed and she is again working her way to becoming a light traveler, this time with a kid.

INTRODUCTION

He who would travel happily
must travel light.

-Antoine de Saint-Exupéry

Travel takes you to different places from seas and mountains to deserts and much more. In your travels you get to interact with different people and their cultures. You will, however, enjoy the sights and interact positively with these new people even more, if you are travelling light.

When you travel light your mind can be free from worry about your belongings. You do not have to spend precious vacation time waiting for your luggage to arrive after a long flight. There is be no chance of your bags going missing and the best part is that you need not pay a fee for checked baggage.

People who have mastered this art of packing light will root for you to take only one carry-on, wherever you go. However, many people can find it really hard to pack light. More so if you are travelling with children. Differentiating between "must have" and "just in case" items is the starting point. There will be ample shopping avenues at your destination which are just waiting to be explored.

This book will show you 'packing' in a new 'light' – pun intended – and help you to embrace light packing practices for all of your future travels.

Off to packing!

DEDICATION

I dedicate this book to all the travel buffs that I know, who have given me great insights into the contents of their backpacks.

THE RIGHT TRAVEL GEAR

1. CHOOSE YOUR TRAVEL GEAR CAREFULLY

While selecting your travel gear, pick items that are light weight, durable and most importantly, easy to carry. There are cases with wheels so you can drag them along – these are usually on the heavy side because of the trolley. Alternatively a backpack that you can carry comfortably on your back, or even a duffel bag that you can carry easily by hand or sling across your body are also great options. Whatever you choose, one thing to keep in mind is that the luggage itself should not weigh a ton, this will give you the flexibility to bring along one extra pair of shoes if you so desire.

2. CARRY THE MINIMUM NUMBER OF BAGS

Selecting light weight luggage is not everything. You need to restrict the number of bags you carry as well. One carry-on size bag is ideal for light travel. Most carriers allow one cabin baggage plus one purse, handbag or camera bag as long as it slides under the seat in front. So technically, you can carry two items of luggage without checking them in.

3. PACK ONE EXTRA BAG

Always pack one extra empty bag along with your essential items. This could be a very light weight duffel bag or even a sturdy tote bag which takes up minimal space. In the event that you end up buying a lot of souvenirs, you already have a handy bag to stuff all that into and do not have to spend time hunting for an appropriate bag.

I'm very strict with my packing and have everything in its right place. I never change a rule. I hardly use anything in the hotel room. I wheel my own wardrobe in and that's it.

Charlie Watts

CLOTHES & ACCESSORIES

4. PLAN AHEAD

Figure out in advance what you plan to do on your trip. That will help you to pick that one dress you need for the occasion. If you are going to attend a wedding then you have to carry formal wear. If not, you can ditch the gown for something lighter that will be comfortable during long walks or on the beach.

5. WEAR THAT JACKET

Remember that wearing items will not add extra luggage for your air travel. So wear that bulky jacket that you plan to carry for your trip. This saves space and can also help keep you warm during the chilly flight.

6. MIX AND MATCH

Carry clothes that can be interchangeably used to reinvent your look. Find one top that goes well with a couple of pairs of pants or skirts. Use tops, shirts and jackets wisely along with other accessories like a scarf or a stole to create a new look.

7. CHOOSE YOUR FABRIC WISELY

Stuffing clothes in cramped bags definitely takes its toll which results in wrinkles. It is best to carry wrinkle free, synthetic clothes or merino tops. This will eliminate the need for that small iron you usually bring along.

8. DITCH CLOTHES PACK UNDERWEAR

Pack more underwear and socks. These are the things that will give you a fresh feel even if you do not get a chance to wear fresh clothes. Moreover these are easy to wash and can be dried inside the hotel room itself.

9. CHOOSE DARK OVER LIGHT

While picking your clothes choose dark coloured ones. They are easy to colour coordinate and can last longer before needing a wash. Accidental food spills and dirt from the road are less visible on darker clothes.

10. WEAR YOUR JEANS

Take only one pair of Jeans with you, which you should wear on the flight. Remember to pick a pair that can be worn for sightseeing trips and is equally eloquent for dinner. You can add variety by adding light weight cargoes and chinos.

11. CARRY SMART ACCESSORIES

The right accessory can give you a fresh look even with the same old dress. An intelligent neck-piece, a couple of bright scarves, stoles or a sarong can be used in a number of ways to add variety to your clothing. These light weight beauties can double up as a nursing cover, a light blanket, beach wear, a modesty cover for visiting places of worship, and also makes for an enthralling game of peek-a-boo.

12. LEARN TO FOLD YOUR GARMENTS

Seasoned travellers all swear by rolling their clothes for compact and wrinkle free packing. Bundle packing, where you roll the clothes around a central object as if tying it up, is also a popular method of compact and wrinkle free packing. Stacking folded clothes one on top of another is a big no-no as it makes creases extreme and they are difficult to get rid of without ironing.

13. WASH YOUR DIRTY LAUNDRY

One of the ways to avoid carrying loads of clothes is to wash the clothes you carry. At some places you might get to use the laundry services or a Laundromat but if you are in a pinch, best solution is to wash them yourself. If that is the plan then carrying quick drying clothes is highly recommended, which most often also happen to be the wrinkle free variety.

14. LEAVE THOSE TOWELS BEHIND

Regular towels take up a lot of space, are heavy and take ages to dry out. If you are staying at hotels they will provide you with towels anyway. If you are travelling to a remote place, where the availability of towels look doubtful, carry a light weight travel towel of viscose material to do the job.

15. USE A COMPRESSION BAG

Compression bags are getting lots of recommendation now days from regular travellers. These are useful for saving space in your luggage when you have to pack bulky dresses. While packing for the return trip, get help from the hotel staff to arrange a vacuum cleaner.

FOOTWEAR

16. PUT ON YOUR HIKING BOOTS

If you have plans to go hiking or trekking during your trip, you will need those bulky hiking boots. The best way to carry them is to wear them on flight to save space and luggage weight. You can remove the boots once inside and be comfortable in your socks.

17. PICKING THE RIGHT SHOES

Shoes are often the bulkiest items, along with being the dainty if you are a female. They need care and take up a lot of space in your luggage. It is advisable therefore to pick shoes very carefully. If you plan to do a lot of walking and site seeing, then wearing a pair of comfortable walking shoes are a must. For more formal occasions you can carry durable, light weight flats which will not take up much space.

18. STUFF SHOES

If you happen to pack a pair of shoes, ensure you utilize their hollow insides. Tuck small items like rolled up socks or belts to save space. They will also be easy to find.

TOILETRIES

19. STASHING TOILETRIES

Carry only absolute necessities. Airline rules dictate
that for one carry-on bag, liquids and gels must be in
3.4 ounce (100ml) bottles or less, and must be packed
in a one quart zip-lock bag. If you are planning to stay
in a hotel, the basic things will be provided for you.
It's best is to buy the rest from the local market at
your destination.

20. TAKE ALONG TAMPONS

Tampons are a hard to find item in a lot of countries.
Figure out how many you need and pack accordingly.
For longer stays you can buy them online and have
them delivered to where you are staying.

21. GET PAMPERED BEFORE YOU TRAVEL

Some avid travellers suggest getting a pedicure and
manicure just the day before travelling. This not only
gives you a well kept look, you also save the trouble
of packing nail polish. Remember, every little bit of
weight reduced adds up.

ELECTRONICS

22. LUGGING ALONG ELECTRONICS

Electronics have a large role to play in our lives today. Most of us cannot imagine our lives away from our phones, laptops or tablets. However while travelling, one must consider the amount of weight these electronics add to our luggage. Thankfully smart phones come along with all the essentials tools like a camera, email access, picture editing tools and more. They are smart to the point of eliminating the need to carry multiple gadgets. Choose a smart phone that suits all your requirements and travel with the world in your palms or pocket.

23. REDUCE THE NUMBER OF CHARGERS

If you do travel with multiple electronic devices, you will have to bear the additional burden of carrying all their chargers too. Check if a single charger can be used for multiple devices. You might also consider investing in a pocket charger. These small devices support multiple devices while keeping you charged on the go.

24. TRAVEL FRIENDLY APPS

Along with smart phones come numerous apps, which are immensely helpful in our travels. You name it and you have an app for it at hand – take pictures, sharing with friends and family, torch to light dark roads, maps, checking flight/train times, find hotels and many other things. Use these smart alternatives to traditional items like books to eliminate weight and save space.

I get ideas about what's essential when packing my suitcase.

-Diane von Furstenberg

TRAVELLING WITH KIDS

25. BRING ALONG THE STROLLER

Kids might enjoy walking for a while but they soon tire out and a stroller is the just the right thing for them to rest in while you continue your tour. Strollers also double duty as a luggage carrier and shopping bag holder. Remember to pick a light weight, easy to handle brand of stroller. Better yet, find out in advance if you can rent a stroller at your destination.

26. BRING ONLY ENOUGH DIAPERS FOR YOUR TRIP

Diapers take up a lot of space and add to the weight of your luggage. Therefore it is advisable to carry just enough diapers to last through the trip and a few for afterwards, till you buy fresh stock at your destination. Unless of course you are travelling to a really remote area, in which case you have no choice but to carry the load. Otherwise diapers are something you will find pretty easily.

27. TAKE ONLY A COUPLE OF TOYS

Children are easily attracted by new things in their environment. While travelling they will find numerous 'new' objects to scrutinize and play with. Packing just one favorite toy is enough, or if there is no favorite toy leave out all of them in favor of stories or imaginary games.

28. CARRY KID FRIENDLY SNACKS

Create a small snack counter in your bag to store away quick bites for those sudden hunger pangs. Depending on the child's age this could include chocolates, raisins, dry fruits, granola bars or biscuits. Also keep a bottle of water handy for your little one.

These things do not add much weight and can be adjusted in a handbag or knapsack.

29. GAMES TO CARRY

Create some travel specific, imaginary games if you have slightly grown up children, like spot the attractions. Keep a coloring book and colors handy for in-flight or hotel time. Apps on your smart phone can keep the children engaged with cartoons and story books. Older children are often entertained by games available on phones or tablets. This cuts the weight of luggage down while keeping the kids entertained.

30. LET THE KIDS CARRY THEIR LOAD

A good thing is to start early sharing of responsibilities. Let your child pick a bag of his or her choice and pack it themselves. Keep tabs on what they are stuffing in their bags by asking if they will be using that item on the trip. It could start out being just an entertainment bag initially but with growing years they will learn to sort the useful from the superfluous. Children as little as four can maneuver a small trolley suitcase like a pro- their experience in pull along toys credit. If you are worried that you may be pulling it for them, you may want to start with a backpack.

31. DECIDE ON LOCATION FOR CHILDREN TO SLEEP

While on a trip you might not always get a crib at your destination, and carrying one will make life all the more difficult. Instead call ahead to see if there are any cribs or roll out beds for children. You may even put blankets on the floor. Weave them a story about camping and they will gladly sleep without any trouble.

32. GET BABY PRODUCTS DELIVERED AT YOUR DESTINATION

If you are absolutely paranoid about not getting your favourite variety of diaper or brand of baby food, check out online stores like amazon.com for services in your destination city. You can buy things online ahead of your travel and get them delivered to your hotel upon arrival.

33. FEEDING NEEDS OF YOUR INFANTS

If you are travelling with a breastfed infant, you save the trouble of carrying bottles and bottle sanitization kits. For special food, or medications, you may need to call ahead to make sure you have a refrigerator where you are staying.

34. FEEDING NEEDS OF YOUR TODDLER

With the progression from infancy to toddler, their dietary requirements too evolve. You will have to pack some snacks for travelling time. Fresh fruits and vegetables can be purchased at your destination. Most of the cities you travel to in whichever part of the world, will have baby food products and formulas, available at the local drug-store or the supermarket.

35. PICKING CLOTHES FOR YOUR BABY

Contrary to popular belief, babies can do without many changes of clothes. At the most pack 2 outfits per day. Pack mix and match type clothes for your little one as well. Pick things which are comfortable to wear and quick to dry.

36. SELECTING SHOES FOR YOUR BABY

Like outfits, kids can make do with two pairs of comfortable shoes. If you can get some water resistant shoes it will be best. To expedite drying wet shoes, you can stuff newspaper in them then wrap them with newspaper and leave them to dry overnight.

37. KEEP ONE CHANGE OF CLOTHES HANDY

Travelling with kids can be tricky. Keep a change of clothes for the kids and mum handy in your purse or tote bag. This takes a bit of space in your hand luggage but comes extremely handy in case there are any accidents or spills.

38. LEAVE BEHIND BABY ACCESSORIES

Baby accessories like their bed, bath tub, car seat, crib etc. should be left at home. Many hotels provide a crib on request, while car seats can be borrowed from friends or rented. Babies can be given a bath in the hotel sink or even in the adult bath tub with a little bit of water. If you bring a few bath toys, they can be used in the bath, pool, and out of water. They can also be sanitized easily in the sink.

39. CARRY A SMALL LOAD OF PLASTIC BAGS

With children around there are chances of a number of soiled clothes and diapers. These plastic bags help to sort the dirt from the clean inside your big bag. These are very light weight and come in handy to other carry stuff as well at times.

PACK WITH A PURPOSE

40. PACKING FOR BUSINESS TRIPS

One neutral-colored suit should suffice. It can be paired with different shirts, ties and accessories for different occasions. One pair of black suit pants could be worn with a matching jacket for the office or with a snazzy top for dinner.

41. PACKING FOR A CRUISE

Most cruises have formal dinners, and that formal dress usually takes up a lot of space. However you might find a tuxedo to rent. For women, a short black dress with multiple accessory options will do the trick.

42. PACKING FOR A LONG TRIP OVER DIFFERENT CLIMATES

The secret packing mantra for travel over multiple climates is layering. Layering traps air around your body creating insulation against the cold. The same light t-shirt that is comfortable in a warmer climate can be the innermost layer in a colder climate.

REDUCE SOME MORE WEIGHT

43. LEAVE PRECIOUS THINGS AT HOME

Things that you would hate to lose or get damaged leave them at home. Precious jewelry, expensive gadgets or dresses, could be anything. You will not require these on your trip. Leave them at home and spare the load on your mind.

44. SEND SOUVENIRS BY MAIL

If you have spent all your money on purchasing souvenirs, carrying them back in the same bag that you brought along would be difficult. Either pack everything in another bag and check it in the airport or get everything shipped to your home. Use an international carrier for a secure transit, but this could be more expensive than the checking fees at the airport.

45. AVOID CARRYING BOOKS

Books equal to weight. There are many reading apps which you can download on your smart phone or tab. Plus there are gadgets like Kindle and Nook that are thinner and lighter alternatives to your regular book.

CHECK, GET, SET, CHECK AGAIN

46. STRATEGIZE BEFORE PACKING

Create a travel list and prepare all that you think you need to carry along. Keep everything on your bed or floor before packing and then think through once again – do I really need that? Any item that meets this question can be avoided. Remove whatever you don't really need and pack the rest.

47. TEST YOUR LUGGAGE

Once you have fully packed for the trip take a test trip with your luggage. Take your bags and go to town for window shopping for an hour. If you enjoy your hour long trip it is good to go, if not, go home and reduce the load some more. Repeat this test till you hit the right weight.

48. ADD A ROLL OF DUCT TAPE

You might wonder why, when this book has been talking about reducing stuff, we're suddenly asking you to pack something totally unusual. This is because when you have limited supplies, duct tape is immensely helpful for small repairs – a broken bag, leaking zip-lock bag, broken sunglasses, you name it and duct tape can fix it, temporarily.

49. LIST OF ESSENTIAL ITEMS

Even though the emphasis is on packing light, there are things which have to be carried for any trip. Here is our list of essentials:

- Passport/Visa or any other ID

- Any other paper work that might be required on a trip like permits, hotel reservation confirmations etc.

- Medicines – all your prescription medicines and emergency kit, especially if you are travelling with children

- Medical or vaccination records

•Money in foreign currency if travelling to a different country

•Tickets- Email or Message them to your phone

50. MAKE THE MOST OF YOUR TRIP

Wherever you are going, whatever you hope to do we encourage you to embrace it whole-heartedly. Take in the scenery, the culture and above all, enjoy your time away from home.

On a long journey even a straw
weighs heavy.

-Spanish Proverb

PACKING AND PLANNING TIPS

A Week before Leaving

- Arrange for someone to take care of pets and water plants.

- Stop mail and newspaper.

- Notify Credit Card companies where you are going.

- Change your thermostat settings.

- Car inspected, oil is changed, and tires have the correct pressure.

- Passports and photo identification is up to date.

- Pay bills.

- Copy important items and download travel Apps.

- Start collecting small bills for tips.

Right Before Leaving

- Clean out refrigerator.

- Empty garbage cans.

- Lock windows.

- Make sure you have the proper identification with you.

- Bring cash for tips.

- Remember travel documents.

- Lock door behind you.

- Remember wallet.

- Unplug items in house and pack chargers.

>TOURIST

READ OTHER
GREATER THAN A TOURIST
BOOKS

Greater Than a Tourist San Miguel de Allende Guanajuato Mexico:
50 Travel Tips from a Local by Tom Peterson

Greater Than a Tourist – Lake George Area New York USA:
 50 Travel Tips from a Local by Janine Hirschklau

Greater Than a Tourist – Monterey California United States:
50 Travel Tips from a Local by Katie Begley

 Greater Than a Tourist – Chanai Crete Greece:
50 Travel Tips from a Local by Dimitra Papagrigoraki

Greater Than a Tourist – The Garden Route Western Cape Province
South Africa: 50 Travel Tips from a Local by Li-Anne McGregor van
Aardt

Greater Than a Tourist – Sevilla Andalusia Spain:
50 Travel Tips from a Local by Gabi Gazon

Greater Than a Tourist – Kota Bharu Kelantan Malaysia:
50 Travel Tips from a Local by Aditi Shukla

Children's Book: Charlie the Cavalier Travels the World by Lisa
Rusczyk

> TOURIST

Visit Greater Than a Tourist for Free Travel Tips
http://GreaterThanATourist.com

Sign up for the Greater Than a Tourist Newsletter for
discount days, new books, and travel information:
http://eepurl.com/cxspyf

Follow us on Facebook for tips, images, and ideas:
https://www.facebook.com/GreaterThanATourist

Follow us on Pinterest for travel tips and ideas:
http://pinterest.com/GreaterThanATourist

Follow us on Instagram for beautiful travel images:
http://Instagram.com/GreaterThanATourist

> TOURIST

Please leave your honest review of this book on Amazon and Goodreads. Please send your feedback to GreaterThanaTourist@gmail.com as we continue to improve the series. We appreciate your positive and constructive feedback. Thank you.

METRIC CONVERSIONS

TEMPERATURE

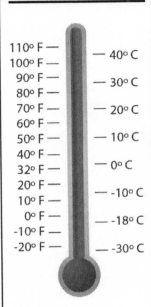

110° F —
100° F —
90° F —
80° F —
70° F —
60° F —
50° F —
40° F —
32° F —
20° F —
10° F —
0° F —
-10° F —
-20° F —

— 40° C
— 30° C
— 20° C
— 10° C
— 0° C
— -10° C
— -18° C
— -30° C

To convert F to C:
Subtract 32, and then multiply by 5/9 or .5555.

To Convert C to F:
Multiply by 1.8 and then add 32.

32F = 0C

LIQUID VOLUME

To Convert:...................Multiply by
U.S. Gallons to Liters................. 3.8
U.S. Liters to Gallons 26
Imperial Gallons to U.S. Gallons 1.2
Imperial Gallons to Liters....... 4.55
Liters to Imperial Gallons 22
1 Liter = .26 U.S. Gallon
1 U.S. Gallon = 3.8 Liters

DISTANCE

To convert ....Multiply by
Inches to Centimeters 2.54
Centimeters to Inches 39
Feet to Meters........................ .3
Meters to Feet 3.28
Yards to Meters 91
Meters to Yards 1.09
Miles to Kilometers 1.61
Kilometers to Miles............ .62
1 Mile = 1.6 km
1 km = .62 Miles

WEIGHT

1 Ounce = .28 Grams
1 Pound = .4555 Kilograms
1 Gram = .04 Ounce
1 Kilogram = 2.2 Pounds

TRAVEL QUESTIONS

- Do you bring presents home to family or friends after a vacation?

- Do you get motion sick?

- Do you have a favorite billboard?

- Do you know what to do if there is a flat tire?

- Do you like a sun roof open?

- Do you like to eat in the car?

- Do you like to wear sun glasses in the car?

- Do you like toppings on your ice cream?

- Do you use public bathrooms?

- Did you bring your cell phone and does it have power?

- Do you have a form of identification with you?

- Have you ever been pulled over by a cop?

- Have you ever given money to a stranger on a road trip?

- Have you ever taken a road trip with animals?

- Have you ever went on a vacation alone?

- Have you ever run out of gas?

- If you could move to any place in the world, where would it be?

- If you could travel anywhere in the world, where would you travel?

- If you could travel in any vehicle, which one would it be?

- If you had three things to wish for from a magic genie, what would they be?

- If you have a driver's license, how many times did it take you to pass the test?

- What are you the most afraid of on vacation?

- What do you want to get away from the most when you are on vacation?

- What foods smells bad to you?

- What item do you bring on ever trip with you away from home?

- What makes you sleepy?

- What song would you love to hear on the radio when you're cruising on the highway?

- What travel job would you want the least?

- What will you miss most while you are away from home?

- What is something you always wanted to try?

- What is the best road side attraction that you ever saw?

- What is the farthest distance you ever biked?

- What is the farthest distance you ever walked?

- What is the weirdest thing you needed to buy while on vacation?

- What is your favorite candy?

- What is your favorite color car?

- What is your favorite family vacation?

- What is your favorite food?

- What is your favorite gas station drink or food?

- What is your favorite license plate design?

- What is your favorite restaurant?

- What is your favorite smell?

- What is your favorite song?

- What is your favorite sound that nature makes?

- What is your favorite thing to bring home from a vacation?

- What is your favorite vacation with friends?

- What is your favorite way to relax?

- Where is the farthest place you ever traveled in a car?

- Where is the farthest place you ever went North, South, East and West?

- Where is your favorite place in the world?

- Who is your favorite singer?

- Who taught you how to drive?

- Who will you miss the most while you are away?

- Who if the first person you will contact when you get to your destination?

- Who brought you on your first vacation?

- Who likes to travel the most in your life?

- Would you rather be hot or cold?

- Would you rather drive above, below, or at the speed limited?

- Would you rather drive on a highway or a back road?

- Would you rather go on a train or a boat?

- Would you rather go to the beach or the woods?

TRAVEL BUCKET LIST

1.

2.

3.

4.

5.

6.

7.

8.

9.

10.

NOTES

Made in the USA
Columbia, SC
28 July 2021